What Do You Call Someone Who Loves Love?

What Do You Call Someone Who Loves Love?

A Love Keeper.

Naura Zdin

PARTRIDGE

A Penguin Random House Company

To order additional copies of this book, contact
Toll Free 800 101 2657 (Singapore)
Toll Free 1 800 81 7340 (Malaysia)
orders.singapore@partridgepublishing.com

www.partridgepublishing.com/singapore

To my One true love, thank you for making me part of something big- this beautiful life which is constantly reminding me that there is beauty in everything.

To the little voice in my heart who told me to follow the quiet beat of my dreams, thank you for not faltering.

To all the people in my life, this one is for you.

Writer's block

---

*I want to write so much about you, in different
symbols, different languages, different characters,
but I just can't seem to fit all of my love for you.*

*Your picture is apparent in my eyes, your name upon my lips,
the memory of you is etched in my heart and soul.*

How then do I start?

Naura Zdin

The quiet happiness

Happiness is the sound of your voice at the end of a long day.
Happiness is the way you say, today is a challenging day
and I'm actually mad at you, but I still love you the same.

Happiness is the way love creeps up at me at the most
helpful time, especially when I miss you most.

Happiness is knowing that I have a beautiful
soul as yours, deeply in love with me.

Naura Zdin

A wonderful kind of odd

---

*What are the odds that you have similar thoughts as me and
we ended up wearing colour-coordinated clothes so often.*

*What are the odds that we prefer eating in silence and
just enjoying our food and presence, but when we have
so much to say, we ended up talking and stopping at the
same time and then breaking out in fits of laughter.*

*How annoyingly simple that we agree on things-
where to eat, what do we do next-
you know that small pesky stuffs that
nobody likes to decide on.*

*What are the odds that the right one just came along
unannounced, looked at me in the eye and said, "tell
me what happened to you" and genuinely meant it.*

Naura Zdin

I miss you secretly

Just remember people say I miss you in different, subtle ways-

"Looking forward to your return",
"Text me when you are safely home",
"So glad to hear from you",

It all means the same thing-
I miss you so.

Naura Zdin

A natural bond

*We were laughing and laughing and the next thing
we knew, we were kissing and we were still laughing,
our fingers entwined, and you know, there was no
better taste than his laughter in my mouth.*

Naura Zdin

Favorite feeling

---

*That warm, unexplainable feeling of how you
always make my day seems better-*

Slowly, then all at once.

Naura Zdin

Period

I love how you send, "I love you" or
"I miss you" to me, and all those love notes
without a period at the end-
like your love for me has no end to it.

Naura Zdin

The shared meal

It was supposed to be just dinner. It lasted for 9 hours and ended off with a hearty breakfast-breakfast with a lot of heart-breakfast with a lot of love.

Naura Zdin

A quiet kind of love

You know the times the sea kisses the shore?

*Perhaps that's how they actually tell each other
how much they miss each other-*

Perhaps that's how much my heart misses yours too.

Naura Zdin

Within 24 hours

---

*I love the way you make me feel from the start
of the day to the end of the night.*

Naura Zdin

While reading

Sometimes you keep re-reading a particular page
just because it reminds you of something-
A place, an event, a date.

Sometimes you stare at the words over and over
again because you are trying to relate, trying to
put your finger to a particular memory.

And sometimes, you just skip the whole sentence
because you never want to go there, you never want
to know the next inevitable thing that is going to
happen- like it will bring you back to the past,
Like you are going to lose someone all over again.

Naura Zdin

Before 12

At the end of the day
I will look for that sentence,
that knowing image,
that gentle laughter-
Anything at all that reminds me of what makes you, you.

Naura Zdin

A familiar morning face

Funny how we see each other every morning but we know nothing of that person. Then we start to notice that person a little bit more- what the person is wearing, how the person is going to get through the day, and you hope that that person is going to have a good day when you locked eyes with them- albeit briefly.

Naura Zdin

0637 hour

I love a warm cup of tea.
I like reading - I'm the type of person who will keep
reading the end of the book just because I like the ending.
I like happy people.
I appreciate solitude.
I think people underestimate kindness and I think
there's no point in worrying for the future because
life has a good way of balancing itself out.
I guess what I'm trying to say is to just keep doing the
things that make us happy and be grateful because
we are exactly where we need to be right now.

Naura Zdin

I am home

That every line
Every verse
Every sentence
Just brings my heart
My soul,
The whole of me closer to
You.

Naura Zdin

More than meets my eye

Look and see where my heart is.
Look closer and you would have realized that
I, for whatever reasons -
maybe brave, or taking a leap of faith,
or both have chosen to put this heart on somebody else's sleeve.

Naura Zdin

Intersection

That
funny
winding
road
where
my
laughter
meets your
laughter.

Naura Zdin

At the moment

Now is beautiful the way it is.
Embracing, still, around.
Right where I need you to be.

Naura Zdin

First point of sight

The thing is,
When I rub my eyes
and roll to the other side,
I hope to find you,
At that moment,
When my eyes are finally ready for the world.

Naura Zdin

An unknown that I know

What if we already know each other
before we even know each other?

It could be that you were
that familiar scent,
that familiar gaze, or
that familiar smile
that I knew so well before I
met

you.

Naura Zdin

Lost and found

"Where were you?" he asked, his heart skipping a beat.

"Just here." she replied.

"I was here. You were nowhere in sight." he said.

*"I was nowhere in sight because I am inside,
right here, in your heart." her heart skipping
to his beat - slow, rhythmic, and placid.*

Naura Zdin

Ease

My hands
S
E
A
M
L
E
S
S
L
Y

finding its way to
yours.

Naura Zdin

Endless cycle

Why is it that when one stays,
The other leaves,
and why is it that when one leaves,
The other tries to catch?

People love to run in circles, don't they?
"How silly."
she thought.

Naura Zdin

A silent force

When I think about it,
I would like to be the wind.
No.
Not the sun,
nor the rainbow,
nor the rain,

but just the wind,
because it never leaves halfway,
it never only appears after the rain,
it never stops giving out love.

It will always remain in a still and quiet
manner, but it never ever leaves.

Naura Zdin

Love like this

A love that makes your heart blossom,
a love that makes your heart flutter,
a love that makes your heart smile,

is a love that never dies.

Naura Zdin

Upon a star

I wish and wish just a little more today
that you could just see you,

Through my eyes.

Naura Zdin

A surprise gift

---

*Sometimes, we try so hard to reach out, try so hard to
hold on to something that is no longer benefiting us
that we sap the life out of it till it almost runs dry.*

*I think we are better off when we figure out that
it is time to let go of something that has no longer
serve its purpose to us. It hurts, stings a little every
now and then but I think it is necessary.*

*If we still try to hold on to something that is
slowly losing its meaning in our life, I think
we would miss out on something bigger-
Something better that is already in store for us.*

Naura Zdin

Kinesthetic

You make me do things which I can't
control whenever you are near me -

Like how my hairs stood up at the back of my neck or how my
hands went in and out of my pockets like it's out of place -

I don't even know what to do with it.

Naura Zdin

A little bit more than try

Sometimes,
try as you might,
you just can't get over it because it changes you from within -

a part of you is not exactly you -
you carry that part of someone with
you for the rest of your life.

Naura Zdin

How do you know

How do you know
that you are in love?

It's when you say the name
And you feel warm all over,
With tingles in your bones
And that the name feels safe, just right,
in your mouth.

Naura Zdin

A dear confession

Dear you,
All that you see of me
is, but just a fringe -
While the rest belongs to love,
While the rest belongs to my One true love.

Naura Zdin

Clear as day

---

*"What do you remember most about him?" A
series of memories flashed through my mind so
fast, an upward curve formed on my lips.*

*I choose to remember all the great things he did, not the other,
for I will always choose love over hate, anytime.*

Naura Zdin

A part of me

How can you run from what's inside you, living within you, and breathing just underneath your skin?

Naura Zdin

Lesson 101

I have met so many people in my life that
have made me fall in love.
But you,
You were my favourite because you have taught
me to fall in love with me first.

Naura Zdin

Presence

Just like how the morning breaks and spreads its grace,
That is how you are to me and so much more, always more.

Naura Zdin

Camera trick

I think of you in a hundred little ways.
Sometimes I think of you in colours that don't exist,
sometimes in seasons that I don't recognize.

Then I remembered the smile in your
eyes and almost instantaneously,
Your face,
Your smell,
the whole of you came back into focus.

Naura Zdin

Three is not a charm

You are always ahead of me
no matter how hard I try to catch up.
You are always three steps ahead of me
with every step that I take.
You thought you'd make it easy for me
with the quick and abrupt presence that you've made, but
that's where you were wrong because every time you leave-
it always hits me hard on my face and harder on my heart,
it leaves me defenseless,
and it is never less painful every single time.

Naura Zdin

Your Type

Throughout the years of my existence, I've
came across hundreds over kisses-
a kiss on the hand,
a kiss on the heart,
the eyelashes,
a blow kiss,

but you, your type of kiss came in the form of words-
so simple-
like magic.

Naura Zdin

The most important meal of the day

---

*It started of with a slice of you in the morning
and it went uphill from there.*

*And I thought I couldn't get any happier than that, but the
day just kept surprising me that I had to pause to catch my
breath, pinched my cheeks, and secretly exclaimed to myself,
"Stop smiling already."*

Naura Zdin

Bravery

Be brave.
Be brave dear heart to love something to your heart's content.
Spill and let it flow. Let anyone who comes into your life
feel the love in your heart even if it's just a brush of it.

If you have it, flaunt it.

Naura Zdin

On my mark

I am ready for love.

*I am capable of loving another person who comes along,
with all my heart and soul, but I am not seeking him.*

*I think the more I love myself, the more life would bring me
to my other half at the most unexpected time and I know that
when it happens, he would love me back with all his heart.*

Naura Zdin

During a trying time

*In case of emergency, do not run away, do not break down,
do not have a great day because it is not going to be.*

Instead, keep faith.

*Breathe, put on your favorite clothes, wear your
nice smile, and don't give up just yet because
eventually things will work their way out.
Until then, keep faith.*

Naura Zdin

An account of you

Maybe if I love you less, I might be able to
talk more about you to people but,
I don't want to love you less.
I want to love you more and more, and let my heart
be filled to the brim with the thoughts of you.

Naura Zdin

A loving hope

I hope that you will fall in love with someone who would
take you to the parks, the museums, or the beaches.

I hope that you will fall in love with someone
who'd pull you into the rain;
run with you, twirl you around, and kiss you in the rain.

I hope that you will fall in love with someone
who would smell the flowers, pluck one of its
stem and hook it into your beautiful hair.

I hope that you will fall in love with someone who would
do anything just to see the smile on your face but more than
that, I hope that you will fall in love with someone who is
not afraid to reel you in whenever you need a safety net to
fall back on, someone who is not afraid to tell you that you've
made a mistake just because he expects only the best from you,
and especially someone who would talk
to the One above about you.

Naura Zdin

Instant connection

I think it's amazing how somehow, somewhere, our paths
were destined to cross, but what makes it amazing is how
effortlessly simple you made me smile just by exchanging
a few simple words with me the first time we met.

Naura Zdin

Between the sand and the shore

You know the times when the waves hit the shore? The time when it's about to roll back into the sea, it grabs itself against the sand not wanting to slip back into the ocean-

That's how much I want to grab you and hold you close, not wanting to let you slip away.

Naura Zdin

Goodnight

I kind of like going to sleep because that's the place
where I get to see you and if I'm lucky, you would
even give me that half smirk or is that a half smile?

I don't know which I like better but you make me smile
that sheepish grin whenever my mind wanders off to you.

Naura Zdin

Keep it simple

Don't you think it is so much easier to feel than to say,
so much easier to laugh than to cry and,
so much easier to listen than to refute?

Don't you think it is so much easier to do the simpler
things but why do we always choose the other?

Naura Zdin

On your own

You cannot control the harsh comments people heap on you or the unfair ways people treat you. People would always have something to say, something to do that may be distasteful.

You can, however,
control how you react to certain things, how you respond to what is being said to you, how you protest and stand your ground without losing your self-respect.

Exercise it.
Create a personal area for positive growth so that you can produce loving vibes and let it radiate to those around you. It is okay but more than that, you deserve to live such a life.

Naura Zdin

A heart full of love

I love laughters.
I love it when people laugh on donuts, peanut butter
or cheese sticks. I love a baby's gurgling chuckle, or
is that a secret language that only babies know?

I love urgency.
I love it when people gave that tiny gasp when their
character died in a story, and I love that panic
look when people woke up just a little too late.

I love mess.
I love dishevelled hair, a child's nondescript
handwriting on the wall, an unmade bed.

I love love.
I love it when it suddenly dawned on someone that
they are in love and I particularly love it when
people steal loving glances at their other half.

I love cries, surprises, exasperation,
accomplishments, and all things in between.

Honestly,
I love noticing on people's emotions just because
there is something pure and intriguing about it.

Naura Zdin

A little stretch

---

*Have you ever wished that you could stretch an
hour maybe even a minute just so you could stay
in that moment that makes you truly happy?*

Naura Zdin

The wrong kind of right

Maybe we have seen each other across a space.
Maybe we have walked along the same path, shared
the same memories, or wished upon the same star.

Maybe that was all there was and that you and
I were just soul mates who did not belong to
each other. Maybe we belonged to each other for
the wrong reasons to make our lives right.

Naura Zdin

Lucky ones

---

*Could it be that we are the lucky ones to be
in this slow, this adventurous trip where my
eyes danced every time it met yours?*

Naura Zdin

Your end of the day

You could be my book, or possibly my pillow.
You could even be my tea, the last thing I
have before I go to bed at night.

I just want you to end the day with me so I think I
want to be your blanket - the last thing that hugs you
and envelopes you in warmth every single night.

Naura Zdin

See you soon

---

*I honestly believe that when I lose
someone, I haven't actually lost it.*

*Instead, I think I'm just letting it go back to the
Creator of love for an even bigger purpose - for
him to keep you in His warm embrace.*

Naura Zdin

Within these four walls

Love is to be at peace with someone within the four walls.
Especially when things get tricky, you don't find
yourself muttering your dissatisfaction about
that person under your breathe and you don't
feel annoyed with that person's proximity.

You feel contented, even fortunate when that person
is around you, be it downstairs or upstairs, sitting
on the couch or lying on the same bed with you.

You still go around doing the usual things you both
do around each other. You feel the same kind of
affection that you are so familiar with, with that
person and your heart is simply at peace.

That is what love is all about.

Naura Zdin

The stranger

Strange, the stranger doesn't seem so strange anymore.

. . . .

She suddenly realized that she could
love him for a long, long time.

Naura Zdin

Sincerity

There is an "I love you enough to remind you to love Him first" behind the message, "it's 7.15 pm already, do what you have to do okay?"

Naura Zdin

A partner

---

*More than just a friend, he is someone whom you can talk to
about anything under the sun, he is not just your close friend,
he is someone who cares for you, sometimes a little too much,
you'd think "Wow, someone actually loves me that much?"*

*A constant comfort in your life-
He gets you. He knows your laughter spots,
your awkward little dance, your favourite
words and he'll even start mirroring it.*

*Someone who not only accepts you for who you are, but
someone who sincerely wants to discover layers after
layers of your being and actually stays by you even after
realizing that you may not be so love-able on some days.*

Naura Zdin

Magnetic

The feeling of his silent gaze on me whenever I look away,

the ridiculous sentences that come out from his mouth,

the hug that swallows me whole and, his brilliant patience when dealing with me or any sensitive situations.

I am utterly and completely in awe.

Naura Zdin

A good day

When I've made your frown turned upside down,
or my existence has caused a stir of joy in your
heart, that is when I have a good day.

Naura Zdin

In a secret garden

A state of being happier than happy is the feeling of
having a comfortable conversation with someone.
Silence becomes comfortable.
Losing time with each other is a delight.

You don't want to sleep,
you become wide awake with each passing time and,
you feel blessed because of this thing called love.

Naura Zdin

In all honesty

I love you because He has gifted you to me.
I love you because He loves you,
and I love you because of the things that you
do to remind me of His love for us.

Naura Zdin

Soft spot

---

*You know what gets to me? What warms my heart?
It's your laughter, the twinkle in your eyes, and your
gaze on me when you thought I didn't notice.*

Naura Zdin

Spoilt for choice

That meaningful glance,
that funny smile.
No, it's that hearty laugh.

But when I think about it,
it's actually a toss between that playful
smirk and how he says my name.

Naura Zdin

Meeting your other half

Love is full of surprises.
Love is talking about anything random and then
exclaiming, "What, you too? I thought I was the
only one!" and then rolling your eyes cheekily to the
other person, mumbling, "What a copycat."

Naura Zdin

Selfless love

Love brings about tranquility not inner agony. It allows you to be at peace with your partner and yourself. You never have to fight with someone else, never have to chase, never have to make your life miserable just to please the one you love, because a love that is sincere will always protect the other person's heart like their own.

Naura Zdin

What makes us, us

*As a couple, I think we are unique for our compassion,
for our forgiveness- how we smooth things over, even the
complicated ones, and how we speak highly of each other.*

*Our affinity is unusual because of our love, the kind
of love where we could act like fools, cry our hearts
out in times of despair, and even laugh uncontrollably
till our noses snort and our tummies hurt.*

*The love we have towards each other is ridiculous and
it would never dilute because we try not to rue over
what is missing in our relationship, instead we believe
in our love for the greater good this life has to offer.*

Naura Zdin

Best of him

---

*He is not the type of man who would declare his love
for me to the whole wide world, neither is he the type of
man who would constantly tell me that he loves me.*

*Instead, I was reassured of his love for me when he
squeezes my hand whenever I am feeling anxious.*

*I know he loves me when he lets me sleep in a while
longer in the morning and how he will make our dinner
all by himself when I am feeling under the weather.*

*I know he loves me when he tells the waiter to make my
meal less spicy whenever we are eating out and also when
he finishes up my food for me without complaints.*

*He is telling me he loves me when his face softens
and he holds his gaze a little while longer on
me whenever I am doing something silly.*

*The happy feelings will keep me warm inside
hence, I will keep his love and I will hold on
to it like I have never did to anyone else.*

Naura Zdin

X marks the spot

*Everywhere on the map will always have You in it.
The part where You watched me sleep through the morning
and noon, accompanied me through the evening and listened
to me talk through the night. There I was blabbering away
about the things that You already knew, I cried and laughed
and repeated the same woes over and over again yet you
lovingly listened and continue to cherish our conversation.*

*Sometimes I asked myself where were you when I needed
you the most and if I'm ever going to get a reply from you.*

*The answer is actually yes because You never leave,
never even once left me alone, no matter how
wide I traveled or how far I drifted away.*

Naura Zdin

Never an ending

The mind wanders off to you just because it
reminds me of what it's like before all these -
Placid,
but beautiful, I am waiting for you,
next.

Naura Zdin

Printed in the United States
By Bookmasters